GETTYSBURG

AMERICAN LANDMARKS

Jason Cooper

The Rourke Corporation, Inc.
Vero Beach, Florida 32964

PHOTO CREDITS:
© Gene Ahrens: cover, title page, pages 8, 10, 17; © James P. Rowan: pages 4, 7, 12, 13, 15, 18, 21

CREATIVE SERVICES:
East Coast Studios, Merritt Island, Florida

EDITORIAL SERVICES:
Susan Albury

Library of Congress Cataloging-in-Publication Data

Cooper, Jason, 1942-
    Gettysburg / by Jason Cooper
        p. cm. — (American Landmarks)
    Includes bibliographical references (p. 24) and index.
    Summary: Briefly describes the Civil War battle of Gettysburg, Lincoln's moving speech there, and the present day military park that serves as the memorial.
    ISBN 0-86593-545-9
    1. Gettysburg (Pa.), Battle of, 1863 Juvenile literature. 2. Gettysburg National Military Park (Pa.) Juvenile literature. [1. Gettysburg (Pa.), Battle of, 1863. 2. Gettysburg National Military Park (Pa.)] I. Title. II. Series: Cooper, Jason, 1942- American landmarks.
E475.53.C767 1999
973.7'349—dc21   99-27476
                                                                            CIP

Printed in the USA

TABLE OF CONTENTS

GETTYSBURG NATIONAL MILITARY PARK

Gettysburg is just a small town in Pennsylvania, but it will live forever in America's history.

From July 1 to July 3, 1863, Gettysburg was the **site** (SITE) of a huge and horrible battle. More than 90,000 soldiers from the northern states faced about 70,000 soldiers from the southern states.

A statue of Union General G. K. Warren stands atop Little Round Top at Gettysburg National Military Park.

Gettysburg was the one battle that most helped the North win America's Civil War. Gettysburg stopped General Robert E. Lee and his Confederate Army's **invasion** (in VAY zhun) of the North. After the battle at Gettysburg, the Confederate Army returned to the South.

The price of Gettysburg was terrible for winners and losers alike. The North had 23,000 casualties. The South had as many as 28,000. On a battlefield, a casualty is any soldier who is wounded, killed, or captured. Gettysburg created more casualties than any battle fought in North America.

Civil War battles, like Gettysburg, were often fought in open areas by men close together. They were easy targets.

The Battle of Gettysburg was so important—and so horrible—that President Abraham Lincoln himself came to the battlefield on November 19, 1863. President Lincoln gave a short speech that became known as the Gettysburg Address.

President Lincoln's words honored the men who fought at Gettysburg, especially the thousands who died. He also **dedicated** (deh duh KAYT uhd) a national cemetery at Gettysburg. Most of the Union war dead were buried there. Later, in 1895, the U.S. Congress made much of the battlefield a national military park.

The 17-acre Gettysburg National Cemetery was dedicated by President Abraham Lincoln on November 19, 1863.

BEFORE GETTYSBURG

For years, the northern and southern states had argued about whether states should allow their citizens to hold slaves. They argued, too, about whether new states should be allowed to have slaves.

In the South, big farms called **plantations** (plan TAY shunz) ran on the work done by slaves. Southerners did not want their way of life to end.

Finally, in 1860, southern states began leaving the United States to form their own nation, the Confederate States of America.

E
+
W

Peaceful today, Gettysburg was the scene of vicious warfare. General Robert E. Lee's invasion of Pennsylvania was his last major attack on Union forces in the North.

Lydia Leister's home served as General Meade's headquarters. Meade was named commander of the Union forces just days before the battle.

General George Meade rides his horse in this statue at Gettysburg. Meade's forces permanently crippled the Confederate Army at Gettysburg.

President Lincoln said no state had the right to leave the others. He realized that only force would keep the North and South together. In April 1861, the Civil War between North and South began.

By 1863, several big battles had been fought. The North had more soldiers, factories, and firepower. But the South was holding its own.

In June 1863, General Lee decided to invade the North. He hoped to win a large battle. Then, he thought, the war-weary North might agree to peace.

Big guns made up each side's artillery. In a huge artillery duel on July 3, 1863, the Union answered the Confederacy's 100 guns with 140 pieces of its own.

THE BATTLE OF GETTYSBURG

General Lee marched toward Harrisburg, the capital of Pennsylvania. But as Lee moved into northern territory, the Union Army prepared to stop him.

On June 28, 1863, Lee first learned that General George Meade's Union Army was close. But neither army knew exactly where the other was. On June 30, Union **cavalry** (KAV ul ree) soldiers—men on horseback—discovered Confederate soldiers near Gettysburg. Fighting broke out, and both sides sent for help. By the morning of July 1, both armies were fighting with thousands of men in and around Gettysburg.

16

Statues and monuments erected by northern and southern states remember their fighting men at Gettysburg.

MISSISSIPPI
JULY 1ST 2ND 3RD 1863

ON THE GROUND OUR BRAVE SIRES FOUGHT FOR THEIR RIGHTEOUS CAUSE
IN GLORY THEY SLEEP WHO GAVE TO IT THEIR ALL
TO VALOR THEY GAVE NEW DIMENSIONS OF COURAGE
 . . . BUT ITS NOBLEST FULFILLMENT
. . . THE SACRED HERITAGE OF HONOR

By night, Lee's army had captured 2,500 Union soldiers and pushed the Union Army backward. On July 2 the Union Army bent more, but didn't break.

On July 3, both sides fired cannon shells at each other for seven hours. Afterward, General Lee thought the Union defense might be weak at its center. He sent 13,000 Confederates across open fields to attack. Their brave attack became known as Pickett's Charge.

The Union soldiers were in good positions. They shot at the Confederates from three sides, slaughtering thousands. The next day, General Lee's defeated army returned to Virginia.

The charge against the Union center on July 3, 1863, ended in a slaughter of Confederate soldiers.

THE GETTYSBURG ADDRESS

There were no radios or televisions in 1863. But President Lincoln's two-minute Gettysburg Address was reported by newspapers. It seemed that everyone who heard—or read—the president's words was touched.

President Lincoln remembered in his speech that the founders of the nation said that "all men are created equal." The Civil War, he said, was a test of whether the nation would truly be a land of freedom and equality.

President Lincoln also remembered the soldiers "who gave their lives" so that the "nation might live."

This memorial marks the site of Lincoln's Gettysburg Address.

VISITING GETTYSBURG

An 18-mile (29-kilometer) auto tour at Gettysburg National Military Park leads visitors to important places on the battlefield. The auto tour has 16 stops.

Visitors can also hike on the battlefield trails. The one-mile (1.6-kilometer) Big Round Top loop trail travels past old stone defenses. The nine-mile (14.4-kilometer) Billy Yank trail is the park's longest foot trail.

Monuments and cannons in the park were placed by **veterans'** (VEH tuh runz) groups. They honor the sacrifices of the men who fought at Gettysburg.

GLOSSARY

cavalry (KAV ul ree) — soldiers on horseback

dedicate (deh duh KAYT) — to honor an individual, group, or institution in a public gathering

invasion (in VAY zhun) — the unwanted arrival of outsiders, usually by force; a movement into enemy territory

plantation (plan TAY shun) — a large farm or estate, usually run by people living on the farm

site (SITE) — a place where something is or where something happened

veteran (VEH tuh run) — one who has served in the country's armed forces (military)—army, navy, air force, marines, or coast guard

INDEX

FURTHER READING

Find out more about Gettysburg with these helpful books and information sites:

- Cater, Alden R. *The Civil War.* Franklin Watts, 1992.
- Harness, Cheryl. *Abe Lincoln Goes to Washington,1837-1865.* National Geographic, 1997.
- Johnson, Neil. *Battle of Gettysburg.* Simon and Schuster, 1989.
- Krull, Kathleen. *Lives of the Presidents.* Harcourt Brace, 1998.
- Livingston, Myra Cohn. *Abraham Lincoln: A Man for All the People.* Holiday House, 1993.
- Sandler, Martin W. *Civil War.* Harper Collins, 1996.
- National Park Service on line at www.nps.gov